How to Give Up

How (Exactly) to Let Go & Let God

SHANNON MEDISKY

Illustrations by Margarita Manish
www.etsy.com/shop/PassionPNGcreation

To protect the privacy of certain individuals some names and
identifying details have been changed.

"Let not your hearts be troubled..."

~ Jesus Christ

John 14:1a

CONTENTS

INTRODUCTION

Misery loves company, right? But maybe we don't all want to join a pity party. Instead, maybe we're all looking for help and reaching out to each other with the hope that someone has experience with the same frustration, challenges and strain that stress places on our lives. And maybe—just maybe— someone has figured out a way to make things better.

Let's start by getting something out of the way right away. I did the exact opposite of what a writer is supposed to do. I didn't write about what I know. I wrote about what I desperately needed to learn. I wrote the book I was searching for during one of the most challenging periods of my life but never found. So if you're in the second group of people—those looking to skip out on the pity party to search for concrete ways to make things better—then get comfortable and stay with me.

Let me be very clear upfront about one other thing. In no way do I claim to be an expert on anything. I'm not a theologian. I don't have a PhD or a bunch of letters behind my name. If anything, I'm a struggler. I struggle with stress. I struggle with frustration. I struggle with juggling the different challenges in my life. But, frankly, my biggest struggle has been claiming God's promises of perfect rest, an easy yoke and strength instead of weakness in the midst of it all. I struggled—and honestly still do—to experience all of these things in my daily life. But I haven't given up. This book shares what I've learned not in spite of the struggles, but because of them.

To help you better understand where I'm coming from, let me give you a little peek at where I've been and where I am today...

For many reasons after the birth of our biological son, my husband and I decided to grow our family through adoption. My own disability (psoriatic arthritis), a previous pregnancy riddled with complications and Nate's premature birth all factored into the decision. So we started the long, arduous process of trying to locate an adoption agency that would be a good fit for us.

Our search eventually led us to a small, nonprofit adoption agency very near our home. The adoption process dragged on for two long, arduous years. And as time marched on, so did Mark's development. When he finally landed in my arms forever, Mark was no longer an infant but a full-fledged toddler. We'd conquered mountains of clerical mistakes, fought a corrupt foreign government and painstakingly jumped through too many bureaucratic hoops to count. But the journey didn't end there. It was only the very beginning.

Mark has special needs—a whole lot of them. He has special medical needs including an exceedingly strict diet of no more than 15gm of protein per day. Due to a rare genetic condition, Mark's body is unable process protein. If he eats too much protein, it turns into ammonia in his bloodstream causing severe headaches, painful joints and progressive loss of mental functions. If Mark eats too little protein, his body becomes catabolic, breaking down his own muscle tissue to survive. Mark also struggles with a low IQ (intellectual disability) and several communication disorders. To put it very bluntly, Mark's seen more "ologists" than I ever knew existed.

Many people wonder (and some even come right out and ask) if we knew about Mark's special needs before we started the adoption process. I don't really know how to respond. Truthfully, no, we didn't.

The adoption process is never easy . It's riddled with waiting and countless questions and unknowns, including the overall health of the child at the center of it all. We knew that Mark's birth mother was only 14 years old. But it wasn't until much later that we found out that Mark might have medical challenges and special needs.

We had invested ourselves emotionally and financially for quite some time before the required genetic testing revealed any concerns. (In Guatemala, it was standard practice to verify maternity before a child could be legally adopted.) But, frankly, could I—would I—turn my back on a child who needed a family just because he wasn't perfect? The short answer is no. But it certainly isn't the "easy" answer. I would soon find out that a willing heart wasn't all that would be necessary.

When Mark finally came home, he was a very

broken, hurting little boy. I assumed that time, patience and love would fix things and fix him. But sadly some situations and even people can't be fixed. Sometimes things don't go according to our timing. They don't always work out the way we hope or plan, no matter how hard we try to force them to. And this, unfortunately, was one of those times.

I've been Mark's momma for over 7 years now. I wish I could say he's better physically, but I can't. As time has marched on, Mark's medical and developmental special needs have only continued to grow. New genetic testing has revealed even more challenges and problems that will likely confront Mark and our family.

But that's not the end of the story, not by a long shot. Thankfully, God has been able to weave a beautiful story out of frustration, pain and doubt. But it didn't just happen. God doesn't wave a magic wand and force us into anything. I've had to let Him. I've had to learn (exactly) how to step aside and let God work—an admittedly difficult task for me to do.

This book details exactly how I learned how to do this. It shares the skills I struggled to gain in order to give up, so I could be open to the story that God was writing in the midst of my mess. It's my hope that in honestly sharing my own story and struggles—and the specifics I learned along the way—that I can help make your journey towards giving up a little easier and the load you carry on the way to getting there a bit lighter.

ABOUT THIS BOOK

If you're looking for compelling reasons why you should move over and make more room for God in your life, this book simply isn't it. Go ahead and put it down now. This isn't the book for you.

On the other hand, if you're looking for a book that leaves out all the lengthy lectures about what you should do—you know, all the stuff you already know—and instead skips straight to the stuff you desperately want to learn—like how exactly to do it—then settle in.

I'll be the first to admit it. This book is most definitely not the "touchy-feely" type. That's just not me. Nor is it filled with regurgitated Scripture. (You can likely read and understand the Bible yourself.) What you will find in the following chapters is real, practical, step-by-step, hold-your-hand help that you can apply to experience real, lasting, positive change in your life. (And who doesn't want that?)

I won't promise that the contents of this book will change your life. Only you can do that. But what I will promise is to honor your time by getting straight to the "nitty gritty". I jump right to the good stuff about how exactly to claim—and as a result, experience— all the wonderful promises in the Good Book, the perfect rest, the easy yoke and strength instead of weakness. You get the idea and you've probably read in the Scriptures about these promises hoping to claim them. Well, here's the kicker. God hasn't dropped the ball. We have. But take heart because this book will show you how to get back in the game.

God never meant for life to be difficult. But just as it's human to error, it is also human to muddle things up, to needlessly complicate things—and ultimately, to allow life to crowd God out. I know because I've done it. I shamefully *still* do it. But I've also taken concrete steps to fix it. So settle in to read the (honest) scoop about my own journey towards picking up the ball that God has tossed in my court and how you can also get back in the game—the way that God has always intended.

So, it's time. It's time to give up. And with God's help and more practice, I'm confident that I can become a complete loser before too long. And so can you.

Join me?

FINDING THE CALM

I form light and create darkness,
I make well-being and create calamity,
I am the LORD, who does all these things.
Isaiah 45:6-7

I've always found this particular verse from Isaiah comforting. Knowing that no matter what's going on in my life, no matter what kind of storm I find myself in, no matter what kind of mess I find myself in the middle of, the Lord has His hand in it all.

There's one word in particular, though, that's always jumped out at me: calamity. It means "grievous affliction" or "great disaster," yet there's also another word hidden inside of it. Take away just a few letters and you see another, very different word: calm.

I'll 'fess up. I've creeped into a dark closet. I did this because I didn't want anyone else to know that I was in there. I even remained silent and still while my husband called my name. I had had it. My heart—and my brain—were nearly broke. I crawled into the dark out of self-preservation. I wasn't really hiding from him. I was hiding from our entire situation, if only for a second.

It took only a few minutes, though, for me to realize that hiding out in the closet wasn't the answer. (Though, frankly, it didn't hurt for those few minutes either. We *all* need to get away and catch our breath from time to time.) As I stood there in the dark, I knew that eventually I would have to return to the worries, to the 24/7 work of parenting a child with special needs and to the awful feeling that my best was never going to be quite enough.

But as I pressed my hot forehead against the cool, textured drywall and listened to my husband call out my name, I also realized something else. I wasn't in this situation alone. There was actually help, waiting and calling my name right outside—right in the middle of the very mess I was trying to run away from. All I needed to do was respond by opening the door and receiving it. And—wow!—so it is with God too. All we need do is let go. Give up. And give it to Him. Calm really can be found in the middle of our calamity. We just need to stop shouldering it all alone by ourselves.

It's incredibly easy to fall into the trap of thinking that our lives would be so much better and that we'd be so much more at peace, if we only didn't have so many responsibilities, if things were different or if only there were more hours in the day so that we could fit it all in and finally catch our breath. But it's a trap.

It's a trap because there will always be pressure. There will always be stuff that needs to get done. There will always be less than ideal circumstances to manage. The key is to find—and experience—the calm in the middle of the calamity, right where we are and in the middle of everything we're dealing with. This is simultaneously the puzzle and the prize.

I know from experience the frustration of trying to do this. With each day that goes by, my son slips further and further away. He's no longer the same little boy he was, even a year ago. Due to his many medical conditions, Mark will never grow to be the man I dreamed he would be when we adopted him. His conditions are lifelong with no cure and no treatment other than a severely restricted diet designed to slow down and not eliminate the damage.

And just when I'd finally wrapped my head and heart around all of this, the other shoe dropped. The metabolic condition wasn't the only challenge that Mark's body had to deal with. As new genetic testing became available, we opted to have Mark tested with the hope that we could find some answers that may better equip us to ease his suffering and delay his deterioration. But that's not what we got. And nothing could have prepared us for what we heard next.

No longer were we just facing a handful of medical challenges and questions. We were blown away to learn that Mark has genetic markers for over 370 different autosomal recessive genetic conditions. We'd unceremoniously been told to think zebra, not horse, whenever we heard the hoof beats of new symptoms in Mark.

To be blunt, I felt like I'd been handed a ticking time bomb of heartbreak and disaster with no hope to ease Mark's suffering either now or in the future. And, frankly, it really screwed with my perspective. Where does one find the light when the future seems so bleak, suffocating and dark?

Perspective isn't just a funny thing. It's everything. It filters how we receive information. It focuses how we interpret things, including our own thoughts. It frames how we respond. But most importantly, perspective is something else. It's our choice. And it's a choice that we actively choose every minute of every day. But having just been dealt a heavy blow, there were many times when I felt completely knocked out of place, including knocked out of the proper perspective.

Constantly refocusing and maintaining the proper perspective has been essential to simultaneously working on the puzzle and claiming the prize of peace in the midst of it all. In many ways, it's meant retraining myself and working against my natural inclinations. But it's also meant discovering peace where I never thought it would be possible.

With Jesus' help, all of us can walk on water. We can choose to lose focus, succumb to doubt and drown in the middle of our storms like Peter did. Or we can keep our focus plumb on the proper, true perspective.

It's like a pilot in stormy, dark skies. When they can't see around them, unable to discern right from left, up from down, they become completely dependent on their instruments and they trust solely on their prior training to respond accordingly. They rely on what they *know* is right. They don't depend on what they *feel*. We should, therefore, navigate our own way both in and outside of chaos.

I know that it is far easier said than done, especially when it feels as if you're already running on fumes. But it all comes down to giving up. It comes down to surrendering control—in every single way—so that we can rest in God. His perfect rest is there, just waiting and always within our reach. We just have to somehow find a way to stop struggling so we can recognize and experience His peace instead.

What follows isn't a checklist of things to do. It's a list of ways to affect change inside you and—as a result—change in your life. It provides specific ways to begin to unpack some of the burden you've likely lugged around for way too long. In short, it's a list of ways on how to become a complete loser.

Ready? Get set to stop fighting a losing battle. It's time to start fighting a battle to lose. It's time to fight the good fight, the fight to find —and enjoy—the calm that God always intended you to experience, no matter how your circumstance might scream otherwise.

OUR RELATIONSHIP WITH CONTROL

Are you so busy and overwhelmed that you just don't feel like yourself? It's not your imagination. You're likely not yourself, at least not the you God intended you to be.

God created each of us for a purpose (Proverbs 16:4, Ephesians 2:10). There's so many things He's designed us to do. But ironically, there's one thing we were never created to do in the first place, yet so many of us struggle with it to our detriment: control. So much of our frustration and exhaustion—mental, physical and emotional—boils down to our longing for control.

Poor Eve gets a bad rap. She did what so many of us

do every single day. She plucked and sank her teeth into the forbidden fruit. We also do this when we seek to control our circumstances, wonder why things won't hurry up and improve and when we question why things are the way that they are.

The truth is that God told Adam and Eve what was beneficial for them, but He didn't tell them what to do. He still left the choice up to them. That's why both trees were placed in the garden. Similarly, the choice to chase after control or give everything up to God is our choice. If life were always perfect and there never were any challenges, there wouldn't be much choice for us at all. If we could only tame our appetite!

Know your place.

You can make many plans,
but the LORD's purpose will prevail.
Proverbs 19:21 (NLT)

I just didn't get it. Over the past year, I had relished the opportunity to create an enviable collection of engaging toddler toys. They buzzed and beeped. You could snap, zip and button them. Some of them even recited the A, B, Cs and 1, 2, 3s at the push of a button. But no matter which one I placed in front of Mark, he just sat there. His blank stare confused me. His lack of reaction completely baffled me. *Why wouldn't this kid play?* He was well over three years old. All these colorful toys were age appropriate. It said so right on the box.

It took about a week before I realized that I was getting nowhere. No matter how hard I tried, I just couldn't lure Mark into playing. As I sat in the middle of the living room floor, surrounded by a sea of blinking, battery-operated toys, Mark looked up at me and simply smiled. And that's the precise moment when I finally got it.

All this play stuff I'd accumulated with the very best of intentions just wasn't going to work, at least not for Mark, not now. These toys didn't fit the place where *Mark* was currently at. Sure, he was a toddler. But his chronological age and his developmental age were far apart. I had to start from scratch.

About a day or so later, I discovered that I was absolutely right. Gone were the lacing boards which were replaced with teething beads that his hands could eagerly explore. And forget the alphabet magnets for the fridge. They were quickly replaced with wooden blocks that could be stacked, tumbled and rolled around on the floor.

I had thought that if I provided enough encouragement and stimulating toys, that I could pull Mark along to exactly where he should be developmentally. But I was wrong. No amount of effort, money or wishing on my part could make this so. Instead, I needed to meet Mark's needs right where he was, not where I wanted him to be. I had to know Mark's place in order to truly help him along.

No matter how you feel and how many walls you're hitting, you are also exactly where you're supposed to be. You might have planned otherwise. You might really want to be somewhere else. However, you must understand (and work to accept) that it's not up to us. It can be easy to fall into the emotional trap of feeling cornered, like there's no way out. But when you recognize that you're right where God put you to begin with, you can let go of the negative feelings and sit securely until God wants you elsewhere.

Remember how it felt waiting for Christmas as a kid? Time moves painfully slow. It feels as if it's never going to arrive. Likewise, waiting patiently where we are can be an absolutely agonizing experience. But this is what we're called to do. Don't ruin the beautiful gift God that has waiting for you right where you are by trying to force the timing to get elsewhere. Stop watching the clock. Just be still.

Practical Action:

Being still is scary. It can feel like we're stuck and we're not making progress. But being still enables us to work on us exactly where we are. If God's pressed a pause button on your life, take advantage of it. It's no accident. He's done it on purpose.

Practicing gratitude can do a lot more than just changing our attitude. It can also make being still easier. Each time you find yourself focusing on what you wish was different, identify a specific thing that you wouldn't change. Simply denying that your desires aren't there, won't work. You should retrain your thought habits and create a new pattern instead.

Jealousy isn't just an emotion that we feel towards others. We can also feel it towards our imaginary selves. We can waste considerable time and energy wishing that we were elsewhere and doing other things. But this tug of war of the heart robs us of the peace and progress we can enjoy and make right where we are.

♡ Know your role.

And the peace of God,
which surpasses all understanding,
will guard your hearts and your minds in Christ Jesus.
Philippians 4:7 (ESV)

Sometimes we get to choose our role. For the most part, we get a say in how we make a living. We get to choose our friends. We're able to volunteer for causes and tasks that we enjoy. But sometimes we don't. Sometimes we find ourselves in a role we don't want or—even worse—feel completely ill-equipped for.

I'll never forget those first few months that Mark was with us. He didn't talk. In fact, he barely made any noises at all, not even to cry. He refused to walk. Instead, he'd either reach up to be carried or just remained rooted to the spot. He wouldn't feed himself. He'd just smile with his eyes darting back and forth from me to the food I'd carefully cut into small, bite-sized pieces on his plate.

I played along for a few weeks. I knew that Mark had been severely abused and profoundly neglected as an infant. So I chalked all of his current behaviors up to that. After all, surely I could be understanding and compassionate about all this little guy had already been through. But as time marched on, I began to worry.

I worried that perhaps my love and desire to cater to his every need was crippling him. I had to find a way to both foster his trust while also forcing him to do things for himself. I became very aware of the fact that my pity for him was enabling his helplessness. My role wasn't just to love him. My role as his mother was also to help him become as capable as possible.

Armed with this new realization, I set out to do exactly what I didn't want to do. It was counterintuitive. Of course, I *wanted* to carry him. Suffering from severe malnutrition and an incred-ibly short stature, Mark was teeny tiny. My natural inclination was to spoon-feed him. The poor kid kept stuffing food into his pockets and hiding crackers in his sleeves. But I also knew that I had to accept and take on a new role, which required me to say, "No"—often.

My new role greatly perplexed Mark. We spent a lot—and I do mean a *lot*—of time standing in parking lots since Mark refused to walk. He spent a lot of time watching me eat, unwilling to lift the food to his own mouth. I also spent a lot of time lying. Yes, you read that right. I lied to my kid. I repeatedly pretended that I didn't know what Mark was pointing to. For some of my performances, I honestly deserved an Oscar. Even Nate, my older son, would lose patience and say, "Momma, he's pointing to *that*!" But no matter. I was going to employ any method that I could in an effort to elicit even the slightest sound out of little Mark.

I'm happy to share that all of my efforts—even the lies—paid off. Mark eventually learned his roles too. It was his job to lift the fork to his mouth. He really could make sounds, if he tried. And—much to Mark's own amazement—his legs and feet really did work after all. But none of these incredible moments happened until I came to know my role and until I stopped doing everything. I had to give up so that Mark could do *his* part too.

God created us to do many things. We're creative beings who can support and love one another. He created each of us with unique gifts and skills. We are born with the ability to reason and to make choices. We can—and should—make wise, informed decisions. To do otherwise would be to neglect a very important part of who God created us to be in the first place. But we were never created to control everything.

To put it bluntly, only God is God. So go ahead and give it up. Give up the frustration and any false notions about how it's your job to make things better. It's your job to make the very best choices you can. But anything else is simply not your job. It's not your role. We are created for a purpose and put somewhere to do something orchestrated by God. You should rest in the promise that you know everything you need to know for right now. It is crucial that you know and remember this. Remind yourself of this as often as necessary.

We all crave to feel needed. We all desire true purpose. But it's important to not chase after a false sense of purpose. It's very easy to fall into the trap of thinking that if we work and try harder, we can make things happen. It's true that sometimes we can. But only if those changes were in God's plan in the first place.

Solomon wisely summed it up, *"The end of the matter, all has been heard. Fear God and keep his commandments, for this is the whole duty of man"* (Ecclesiastes 12:13 ESV). Our purpose isn't a self-created one. We've been created to love God and to live in a relationship with Him. We can't do this if we're constantly fighting for the control which simply isn't ours to have.

I've walked Mark through many painful, scary pro-cedures. He has literally and emotionally clung to me for security. Sometimes his grip was so tight, that it turned his gingerbread colored skin snow white. At other times, his focus on me was so anchored and cemented in place, that I could tell he was purposefully blurring everything else around him out. Mark knew where his safety and security was and he wasn't going to let it—me—go for dear life.

This is the passion we need when embracing our role as children of God. We simply can't cling tightly enough to two things. Our loyalty can't be divided. We have to let go of the steering wheel—our need to control—so that we can better cling to God. That's our role and our purpose. Grab it. Hold it. Know it.

℘ Practical Action:

Daily life is busy. It's stressful. The struggle of juggling everything that we manage can leave us exhausted. It's not right and it's certainly not the way that God intended it to be. But how very easy it is to forget our true role as children of God. I know because I do it too.

But we can't know—let alone honor—our true role if we forget it by allowing life to crowd it out. You can conquer this challenge by building in various cues throughout the day to help you to remember and refocus. Whenever you set out to complete a task or make a decision, take a moment to consider how does doing this honor my role as a child of God? How does it show God's love to others? Being purposeful and intent-driven with our actions is the tangible evidence of knowing our role and fulfilling our purpose.

We all learn differently and knowing your particular learning preference can also come in handy when it comes to spiritual growth. Some people learn by doing (kinesthetic), while others learn by hearing and listening. There are others who learn visually. I'm very much the latter. Color, pictures and diagrams help to cement things in my brain so I can make better sense of them. I use this to my advantage.

Whenever I start to feel overwhelmed or defeated, I've noticed that my posture also starts to show it. I'm more likely to slouch, look down, and to scrunch in on myself like I'm retreating into a little cocoon. When I catch myself doing these things, I visualize a crown sitting on my head and I immediately remind myself that my crown's going to fall off if I don't straighten up. (After all, a child of the one true King shouldn't be slouching.) This visual and subsequent thought process doesn't only help my physical stance. It also helps to make changes in my actions, attitude and choices too.

If you're someone who learns best by doing, consider identifying a specific task you already do throughout the day as a reminder to remember your true calling. If you're an auditory learner, think of a sound you hear often or a specific song you can listen to that will help you refocus on your most important role. Whatever your specific mode of learning is, identify it and use it to help you better know, remember and honor your role as a child of God all day, every day and throughout each day.

♡ Respect God's place.

This is the will of the Lord:
Not by might, nor by power, but by my Spirit,
says the LORD of hosts.
Zechariah 4:6 (ESV)

What could be easier than blowing bubbles, right? Wrong. And if you're my kids, *very* wrong. One day, I took Mark and Nate outside to practice this skill. As I watched them quickly and forcibly blow air harder and harder through the small plastic wands, I couldn't help but feel their frustration.

Over and over again, I watched them suck air in only to blow it out twice as hard aimlessly, despite the wand poised carefully right in front of their mouths. Try as they might, their determination and sheer force were also their downfall. They watched in amazement as hundreds of tiny, rainbow orbs poured seemingly effortlessly from my own wand. *What was the difference? Why did mine "work" and not theirs?* It certainly wasn't due to any lack of effort or will on their part.

I gently took the dripping wands from their tiny, sticky hands. Patiently, I demonstrated the art of how to blow gently, steadily, purposefully. It wasn't about how badly they wanted to make bubbles. Their desire couldn't be matched. Neither was it due to any lack of supplies. We were all sharing the same soapy solution and taking turns using the same wands. But no matter how hard I tried to show them, it just didn't work. At least not that day. I couldn't convince them to just slow down. In their innocent enthusiasm, they huffed and puffed but failed miserably in the bubble-blowing department.

I've replayed this memory over and over again in my mind's eye in order to remind myself of a very important lesson. No matter how much I will, want or work to change things, I'm not God. It's not my place. Just as Nate and Mark needed to curb their own enthusiasm in order to actually achieve bubble-blowing success, we all also need to humble ourselves in order to respect God's place.

Giving everything up to God is easy when you remember and respect His place. We can be still when we purpose to know that He is God. He never changes. His role and place above everything always stays the same. We allow life to clamor around us and to drown out this calming truth. Purpose to pause whenever you can and remind yourself of this. It can help turn down the blaring volume of life and bring beautiful silence where there once was none.

Although God is always in control, He never forces our choice. We have free will, including the free will to move over and make room for Him. No one likes a busybody, least of all, God. It is important to stop trying to tackle a job that's not ours to begin with.

Whether it's many things or one just major challenge, it can be hard to give up control. But that's exactly what we need to do if we're going to respect God's place and sovereignty over every aspect of our lives. It means moving beyond just knowing and wanting to do this. It requires taking action. That's how we step out in faith.

ꙮ Practical Action:

By remembering how much God cares for us, we can help make the process of loosening our grip on control easier. No one will trust someone who doesn't have their back. But fortunately, we can know that this isn't the case with God. He always wants what's best for us and will always work for good in all things (Romans 8:28).

It's also vitally important to remember that part of respecting God's place means choosing to place ourselves under His care. We choose whether to work in partnership with or against Him. Respect God's place in your life in the midst of your current struggle by actively placing yourself in His CARE:

Challenge:
Write it down. Name it. What exactly are you struggling with?

Accept:
Write down the specific things you have no control over. Acknowledging, appreciating and ultimately accepting our lack of control is vital to respecting God's sovereignty. God is always in control of everything (Job 12:10, Psalm 22:28), but sometimes He does toss the ball in our court. He wants a response and an action from us. The first step is to

figure out exactly what our choices are.

Respond:
After you've focused in on where you can and can't affect change, consider how you should respond. Take the time to evaluate all of your different options and their consequences. Prepare to activate your faith by putting it in motion with your choices (James 2:22).

Engage:
Engage with God in prayer and action. Express your gratitude for His loving care and control over everything. Humbly ask for strength and discernment as you step out in faith, acting on the various decisions you've previously made (Hebrews 4:16).

♡ Understand that control takes many forms.

For God gave us a spirit not of fear
but of power and love and self-control.
2 Timothy 1:7 (ESV)

I shared earlier that Mark didn't speak when he first joined our family. He didn't make a peep. He cried at the airport when he was placed in my arms for the very first time. No—strike that—he *screamed*. But that was it. As you can imagine, my concern grew with every passing day.

I initially came to the understandable conclusion that maybe Mark had hearing difficulties. Speech is often delayed or adversely affected when hearing is diminished. But this was not the case for Mark. Multiple rounds of testing proved that his hearing was crystal clear.

But as Mark became more comfortable in our home and started motoring around independently, he slowly began to make sounds. He wouldn't do it in front of any of us. He'd only vocalize when he thought he was alone. The sneaky little guy would make a high pitch squeal when something pleased him or would hum softly when he was obviously very involved in an activity.

This cat-and-mouse game of trying to catch Mark making noises was fun at first. Sometimes I'd catch him and announce playfully with a smile, "Oh, so Mark *can* make sounds!" He'd grin and his tiny tummy would bounce in laughter—but there was no sound. His sudden awareness of my presence completely snuffed it out of him.

Many months went by and this little game of hide-and-go-peep didn't only grow old, it grew alarming. Nate was typically developing in every way, yet had very delayed speech. So, I was patient. I tried to quiet my heart and hush the worry. But as time marched on, so did my fears.

Before too long, I did what any concerned parent would do. I hit the Internet, asked around and called the doc. There were still no answers and my little boy was still silent, at least when he knew I was watching him.

Like piecing together a puzzle, I tried to look for clues. I knew that he could vocalize. I'd heard it myself. I knew he had typical and appropriate responses to different things. The pitch of his sounds always seemed to fit whatever it was he was reacting to or involved with. So why did he suddenly clam up around me?! Seriously, if I didn't know any better, I would've taken this personally.

Finally, I'd had it. I was determined to play dirty in an effort to get to the bottom of this. So I enlisted the help of Nate. Nate was only sixteen months older than Mark, but I knew he'd be a willing and capable accomplice. So I charged Nate with his task: Go be as silly as possible. The challenge: Make Mark laugh at all costs. I was curious to see if Mark would vocalize in front of, in response to and in an effort to communicate with Nate—while I hid around the corner.

And wouldn't you know it? It worked. It was immediately obvious. For whatever reason, Mark was able to vocalize, at least sounds anyway. It was fear of doing it in front of me, that kept him silent as a mouse.

Control is insidious. It masquerades as many different things, creating a wide variety of emotional reactions from us—including fear. Control is an unrelenting need for answers, a desire to or efforts towards forcing our own timeline or a longing for a different outcome. Control is the opposite of contentment. It's what robs us of peace.

Even fear can be due to control or the lack of it. Fear rears its ugly head whenever we feel threatened. It doesn't matter if it's real or imagined. We're physiologically hardwired to react when this happens. It's called the fight-or-flight response.

Chemicals such as adrenaline, noradrenaline and cortisol are released into our bloodstream giving us the extra boost of energy we need should fighting be required or if we must flee a dangerous situation. But it only needs to be *perceived* as dangerous. We only need to feel like fighting will be required. This is what makes fear such a powerful emotion. This is exactly why we need to be able to identify and manage it successfully.

Avoid letting control disguised as fear back you into a corner or freeze you up like a deer in the headlights. You always have choices— regardless of the circumstances or how you feel.

When fear threatens to fill you or the need to control begins to consume you, make the conscious choice to believe God rather than how you currently feel. Consider this truth: Doubt was behind the original Fall to begin with.

As recorded in Genesis 3:1 (emphasis mine), Satan said to Eve, *"Did God _actually_ say, 'You shall not eat of any tree in the garden'?"* When Satan said this, he was intentionally trying to plant seeds of doubt in Eve. He didn't want her to trust God. Instead, he wanted her to seek control herself. He wanted her to make her own decisions—entirely outside of God's direction. Don't fall into the same trap. Refuse to follow Eve's lead.

Practical Action:

Whenever a negative or challenging emotion threatens to overwhelm you, take a deep breath and trace its roots back to control. Is it an unrelenting, insatiable desire to know why things are the way they are? Is it a crippling fear of what the future holds? Are you stuck in grief over a tragedy, tough news to take or maybe a mistake you feel is irreparable?

Struggling with these kinds of emotions is unfortunately natural in our current human condition. Even as Jesus became *"sorrowful and troubled"* Himself in Gethsemane (Matthew 26:38 ESV), He warned His disciples to *"watch and pray"* because *"the spirit indeed is willing, but the flesh is weak"* (Matthew 26:41 ESV). We've got it on the very best authority—Jesus Himself—that the struggle is indeed real.

We may not be able to avoid the struggle entirely, but we can learn how to stop the exhausting cycle sooner. After you've successfully figured out how your current emotions relate to control, use specific Scriptures to counteract their hold on you. Surround yourself with them. Put them on sticky notes and place them on mirrors, your fridge or your computer monitor.

Seek out songs that will help remind your heart to remember what you already know. Find a trustworthy friend to share your current thought process with. He or she can help by encouraging you to stay the course as you work to practice self-control not just over your actions, but also over your emotions.

🕊 Understand that the urge to control usually stems from feeling uncomfortable.

So humble yourselves under the mighty power of God,
and at the right time he will lift you up in honor.
Give all your worries and cares to God,
for he cares about you.
1 Peter 5:6-7 (NLT)

Mark and I have spent a great deal of time together in waiting rooms. With the many doctors' visits, therapy sessions and surgical procedures, it's been an inevitable fact of life. And, not surprisingly, these waiting rooms aren't his favorite place. They make him incredibly uncomfortable for good reasons. There's a tremendous number of unknowns and too many variables. *When will they call you back? What will happen when they do? Will it hurt? Will there be shots involved?*

My strategy for simultaneously passing the time and managing Mark's anxiety is simple: distraction. I do everything in my power using everything in the room—and in my purse—to occupy him. In other words, I create tangible activities that Mark *can* control while waiting out what he can't.

This usually works pretty well for both of us as long as my creativity and cell phone battery hold out. But it's not authentic. It's just stalling at best. As soon as his name gets called, his face usually falls and so does the temporary comfort he was enjoying just moments before. Fortunately, though, God doesn't play any such games with us. God doesn't dole out distractions.

To truly rest easy in the Lord, means to be able to experience calm and peace no matter what the chaos and no matter how it may clatter around us. But this is obviously far easier said than done. Like Mark, inside every waiting room he's ever been in, we're vulnerable when we're uncomfortable. We're far more prone to slip into old familiar habits no matter how negative or destructive they may be. The good news is that being able to see these tendencies coming before we slip back into them, is the first step to successfully managing ourselves and actively choosing to give everything up to God.

I hate puzzles. No, I loathe them. But even people who really enjoy them can agree that they take work. They require commitment. They demand patience. No matter how much you will a puzzle to be completed perfectly and quickly, it just doesn't happen that way. This requires accepting a certain level of discomfort. This is also true in our daily lives.

This sense of uneasiness—like many of our less than

desirable feelings—can also be reduced down to control. It's not easy when things don't go as we plan or hope. It's uncomfortable to have to wait on a timing other than our own. It's stressful when we don't know what to do next. As difficult as it is to experience all of this, it's human. It is, unfortunately, our current norm.

Maybe that's where our true struggle lies. It involves accepting our roles as the human beings that God created us to be in the first place. We're not human doers, human controllers or human all-knowers. We're human *beings*. God created us to simply be— to be in a relationship with Him (John 15:14-15), to be followers of Jesus (John 12:25-26), to simply be in love with God with our entire being (Matthew 22:37-38).

But we can't do any of these things until we become comfortable with our lack of control. And we do this by choosing to embrace and practice humility, by trusting the One who *is* in complete control.

Ironically enough, it was my older son and a battered up bike that taught me one of my most important lessons. That's right, I got schooled by my little boy. Imagine my surprise when I went from hopping mad to "Ah ha, now I get it" in a matter of mere seconds.

Nate had just received a brand new bike for his birthday. So when I found it covered in scratches, beat up and plastered in torn up blades of grass, you can imagine that I wasn't too happy. We'd spent a tidy sum of money on that bike. Why in the world wasn't he taking better care of it?

The moment I looked out the window and watched him crash into the curb once more was also the moment I'd had enough. I immediately threw open the front door and demanded to know what in the world he was doing.

"But, Momma," he said with a smile. "I gotta learn how to fall too..."

I was left speechless because he couldn't be more right.

We all need to learn how to fall. We need to develop a comfortability with being uncomfortable. We need to learn how to accept a certain amount of discord and—more importantly—how to respond instead of simply reacting to it. After all, we're human. We're still living in the world corrupted and broken because of sin. We still feel the tug of temptation. But as Paul shared, we're called to act differently despite it all (Romans 12:1-2).

It's only natural to reach out for control when we

begin to feel uncomfortable, especially when we have the ability and capacity to change something for the better. And when we can, we should improve things. When it is our place, we should always strive to make things better.

But sometimes it's not our place. Sometimes our place—no matter how much we may wish it differently—is smackdab in the middle of something that's anything but comfortable. Frankly, God's Word tells us this. It should come as no surprise. Sometimes God places us where we *need* to be, not necessarily where we'd *like* to be.

Take Moses, for example. We often think about him as a strong leader, following God and successfully leading the Israelites out of Egypt. But stop for a moment and consider how difficult it must have been for him. God placed Moses in a position where he needed to be, but Moses was far from comfortable with it. He heard the very voice of God tell him exactly what to do, yet he asked, "*Who am I*" to do this? (Exodus 3:11 ESV). God's response wasn't about Moses. Instead, God replied, "*But I will be with you*" (Exodus 3:12 ESV).

When we find ourselves in uncomfortable, challenging situations, we can take our cue from Moses and claim the same comfort too. God is with us just as

He promised to be with Moses (James 4:8). And when Moses stepped up to do what God told him, he didn't struggle for control. He didn't waver or try to control the situation himself by bartering back and forth with the Pharaoh. Instead, Moses stood strong on what God had told him and asked him to do. And no matter how uncomfortable we feel, we can use what we know—what's taught to us in God's Word and the very fact that God is with us—to do the same.

⌘ Practical Action:

Don't buckle and give in to the urge to control. Instead, recognize that you can control it. You can choose to become more comfortable with being uncomfortable. Yes, you read that right. It's not easy. It takes work. It takes practice. But it is possible. And we have the very best Teacher at our immediate disposal to learn from.

Jesus was simultaneously fully God and fully human. He was always fully God (John 8:58, 10:30), but He chose to humble Himself and take on human form (John 1:14, Philippians 2:8). For this reason, we can know that God really does understand our struggles (Hebrews 4:15). And we can look to the example

Jesus set for us to follow—including how to manage our response to feeling uncomfortable.

The most obvious example is Jesus' prayer in the garden of Gethsemane the night before the crucifixion. Tradition has it that Luke, one of Jesus' disciples, was the author of the Gospel that bears his name. It's not too surprising then that the book of Luke, likely written by a doctor (Colossians 4:14), gives the most physical description of Jesus while He prayed that night.

In Luke 22, it tells us that *"being in an agony he [Jesus] prayed more earnestly; and his sweat became like great drops of blood falling down to the ground"* (Luke 22:44 ESV). To say that Jesus was uncomfortable is a severe understatement.

During those moments, He was likely experiencing hematridosis. It's a rare but very real condition that happens when tiny blood vessels that surround sweat glands burst, causing blood to mix with a person's sweat. While the actual cause of hematridosis is still unclear, some scientist believe that it happens when someone is under extreme stress. In Jesus' case, the Gospels overwhelmingly support that He was feeling this way (Matthew 26:38, Mark 14:34, Luke 22:44).

Clearly no amount of our own stress and our own struggles with feeling unsettled can ever come close to what Jesus must have been feeling on that night. But we can take our cue from how Jesus responded. We can follow His lead and choose to do what He choose to do. He did three specific things:

1) Jesus prayed even more fervently.

2) No matter how *"distressed and troubled"* He became (Mark 14:33 ESV), Jesus never wavered from what the Father had called Him to do (Luke 22:42).

3) Jesus focused intently on praying for and caring for others (John 17).

An easy way to remember this, in the midst of our own struggles, is to pray, stay and look away:

Pray in the midst of feeling uncomfortable just as Jesus did. Practice praying everywhere. Remember that prayer doesn't have to be formal, but it should be frequent (1 Thessalonians 5:17).

Stay strong in what we know. We can anchor ourselves to what we know is true so that we're less tempted to get swept away, caught up in and confused by what we don't (Colossians 3:2, Romans 8:5).

Look away from yourself and your present circumstances. Instead, focus on God (Psalm 1:1-3), your relationship with Him (Proverbs 8:17) and how you can love Him by showing His love to others (John 13:34, 1 John 4:11). Our attention should never be too keenly focused on ourselves. To put it bluntly, distraction works. Take the focus off your own uneasiness by purposefully working to help someone else in any way you can.

HOW (EXACTLY) TO GIVE UP

Knowing God is in control is one thing. Actively living that knowledge out in our daily lives is an entirely different proposition. So how exactly can we go from talk to action and from knowledge to application? While it's not always easy, it is thankfully simple. We can do it step by step and bit by bit. Thankfully, God is exceedingly patient with us (Exodus 34:6, 2 Peter 3:9). We just need to also learn how to be patient with ourselves.

Use the ideas below to get the ball rolling. Before you know it, you'll be well on your way to being a complete loser. You have absolutely everything to gain.

🦉 Get to know who's got this. Know He's Got You too!

Fear not, for I have redeemed you;
I have called you by name, you are mine.
Isaiah 43:1b (ESV)

Due to the political and civil unrest in Guatemala at the time, we were strongly advised against traveling there to bring Mark home. So instead an in-country escort traveled the many hours and manned the late night flights and transfers with Mark in tow. At the end of their grueling 19 hours of travel, I finally met my new little boy for the very first time inside a loud, bustling airport.

I strained to sneak my first peek of Mark in person. I did see a very small little boy walking towards us, but quickly dismissed him thinking he was far too tiny to be the two-and-half year old boy we were expecting. I kept looking and looking. But no other children followed. "My God," I thought. "He's *so* small."

By the time he reached us, he was crying uncontrollably. Nate and I had created several brightly colored welcome banners and purchased a few balloons in the hopes of making Mark's homecoming a happy one. But oh how very naïve I was.

This poor kid was tired, hungry, stinky, sweaty and miserable. And I was immediately filled with extreme guilt.

"May I?" I cautiously asked Arella, Mark's escort, as I reached out to take Mark from her arms. She was rattling the words "New Mommy" in Spanish to Mark, as she tried desperately to hush and calm him.

"Yes, you must," she responded both assertively and reassuringly. I was comforted by this. She knew my role. She also knew I was clearly uneasy about jumping right into it. I didn't feel that it was my place. Granted, I was legally his mother, but this frightened little boy didn't know me from anyone else wandering around this cold, gray airport. Both Lupita, our adoption attorney, and Arella chanted reassuring words quietly in Spanish in an effort to help calm and quiet Mark's relentless screams. He only reached back for Arella once, then clung to my shirt, his tiny fists white and tight as if determined to create new wrinkles everywhere.

I held his unbelievably small body facing mine, trying to protect him from the unfamiliar surroundings. But the reality was that I was just as unfamiliar. Despite the fact that I was now his mother, all of the hours spent over webcam singing and playing with him over the past two years and all of the pictures I had sent, I was a complete and total stranger to Mark. And here he was crying, terrified and being forced into my arms. My heart broke and I—once again—felt extreme guilt.

Like Mark, none of us can trust who we don't know. Letting go of everything can be a very scary thing. It's far easier, though, when we get better acquainted with the One who is in control. And we can do this like we get to know anyone else. We can spend time with Him by praying. And we can learn how God has treated others by reading the Bible with an eye bent towards the people, their struggles, their short-comings and how God ultimately related with them.

When Mark first arrived in our home, it wasn't long before we started finding scraps of food hidden inside his little pockets. Sometimes he wouldn't even eat at all, opting instead to secretly stow it away for later—later when he feared the food suddenly wouldn't be around anymore.

Adopted as a toddler, this was unfortunately some-thing Mark was all too familiar with it. Food hadn't always been available. Mark could never trust if there would indeed be food later. His most basic needs for physical comfort hadn't always been readily met. He didn't know us, so he didn't have any reason to trust that things would be different.

It understandably took Mark time to get to know us and to trust that we would faithfully care for him. It was a while before I stopped finding crumbles of food hidden in his clothing. But I was patient with the tucked away food and crumb-filled pockets, understanding that trust takes time and experience to build. God is patient with us too. And He's provided ample ways for us to get to know Him and ultimately appreciate that He's got this—and He's got us too.

Part of fully appreciating that God's got this means being open to and accepting of how He works. We won't always like what happens. It won't always be comfortable. It won't always be fun. But instead of digging our heels in the sand and standing against God's ways, we can bury our heads in His Word and let our hearts rest easy in how He's handled things before.

℘ **Practical Action:**

It's pretty simple, really. We can mind our own business. We can avoid the arrogance and audacity of thinking we can do things better than God. This is very important to understand because our actions and choices often speak louder than our words. Very few of us would actually come out and say that we know or can do better than God, but are our actions and choices saying this for us?

When we're feeling tempted to reach for control or called into the chaos of worry and anxiety, we can refocus our efforts back to who we are. We're human *beings*. It's okay to just *be*. It's our place to simply be—be where God places us, be there for the duration of His timing, be peace-filled in the knowledge that God's got it all—including us.

But like many things, this can be much harder to practice than to simply know. Ironically, I've had to practice just being a lot. Paul's words in his letter to the church in Philippi has also really helped me to devise a concrete way to do it.

Specifically, I take five based on Philippians 4:8. I force myself to take a short break. I take 5 deep breathes and with each one I remind myself of the following:

1. **What is true?**
   God's sovereignty
   (Psalm 115:3, Zechariah 4:6)

2. **What is honorable?**
   Doing everything to the glory of God
   (1Corinthians 10:31)

3. **What is just?**
   Submitting to God's way, will and timing
   (Proverbs 11:2)

4. **What is pure?**
   Maintaining a clean heart
   (Psalm 51:10, James 1:27b)

5. **What is lovely?**
   Putting fear and worry in its place—
   outside of our hearts, so there's more room for
   the fullness of God's love (1 John 4:18)

It's hard to let go, even when we know we should and even when we know that God does have everything under His control. Our emotions often urge us to react. But by purposefully stopping and refocusing, we can resist the urge to react impulsively and instead choose to thoughtfully and carefully respond. We can ensure that our actions and our emotional responses better match what we know and believe.

♡ Trust in His track record.

He will guard the feet of his faithful ones...
1 Samuel 2:9a (ESV)

Even though Mark didn't join our family until well after his infancy, I didn't want him to ever feel like his life didn't start until that point. He was a newborn and had first and second birthdays like everyone else. He also had people who looked after him during that time.

I anticipated well beforehand that Mark would likely have many questions as he grew up. *What did I look like when I was little? Did I have a favorite toy? What did my first set of teeth look like?* So I came up with a plan. Every few months, I mailed a disposable camera to Mark's foster mom.

I asked that she take photos of Mark whenever she could, and not just during the special "landmark" moments. I also wanted day-to-day pictures of Mark. I needed her to document all of this for me so that I could give this precious and irreplaceable gift to Mark, when the moment came.

When we picked Mark up from the airport, he came with nothing but the clothes on his back, a few disposable diapers and—thankfully—a gallon sized bag filled with the disposable cameras I'd sent through the years.

The moment I had so carefully planned for finally came. When Mark was about four years old, he quietly asked me, "Where I come from, Momma? Where be my baby pictures?" I was both grateful and scared. I was so pleased that I had prepared well in advance for this exact moment. But I was also worried, that seeing the pictures would bring back a flood of memories for him and open a flood gate of even more questions, including questions I wasn't yet prepared to answer.

As Mark watched intently, I slid open his closet door and reached for a box perched way up on the top shelf. I handed him the bright red photo album that featured the very first picture I ever saw of Mark right on the cover. Mark grasped it carefully yet eagerly and ran over to his bed.

I watched silently as he flipped slowly, page by page. My eyes couldn't help but well up as I saw a tiny smile make its way across his face. He was obviously comforted by the fact that he was just like his brother, Nate. Sure, he was adopted. But he was born, loved and cared for too, even before he joined our family.

"Who that be, Momma?" Mark asked pointing to the same woman who appeared again and again through-out the album, always holding, hugging and kissing Mark's tiny baby cheek.

"That's your foster mom. We hired her to take good care of you until you could come home," I answered. I was careful to leave out the fact that we had demanded a reassignment to another foster home as soon as we accepted Mark's referral for adoption. His previous placement had been horribly neglectful and most likely abusive. Despite being paid for Mark's care by the in-country adoption agency, Mark had clearly not been fed properly. Later it all became clear. The woman had been taking the money and feeding her own children, but not little Mark.

"I 'member that toy! Where that come from?" Mark asked while pointing to another picture.

"Those are toys I sent you while you grew. I wanted you to have things to cuddle and play with," I replied gently.

"And nice clothes, Momma. I like me pants!" Mark exclaimed proudly pointing to yet another photo.

"Yep, I sent you clothes and new shoes every few months. I always wanted you to feel comfortable and look handsome."

As I uttered this last explanation, God whispered something to my heart too. These pictures weren't just evidence of the life Mark had before landing in my arms. They were clear and indisputable evidence of my care for Mark all along. And suddenly, my tears began to overflow.

Do you wonder how in the world God's gonna get you out of this mess? Are you worried that things are only going to get worse? Stop wringing your hands and start calming your fears by reviewing God's track record. His resume is at our immediate disposal. God's an open book. We just have to review it, pour over it and trust it. We may not know or understand the specifics of His plan, but God and how He works needn't be a complete mystery either. He wants us to trust and peacefully rest in Him (John 16:33), and so He's provided a way for us to get to know Him—through the life of Jesus Christ and through His written Word (Romans 10:17).

✎ Practical Action:

We can read and study the Bible. We can know the Gospels inside and out. We can even spout out verses committed to our memory. But none of this will effect change in our lives unless we truly trust what it means. Trust isn't just a feeling. It's a choice. It's a choice that's followed up by action. We need to take everything we know about God's Word and Jesus' life and act on it.

Have you ever felt stuck? Have you ever felt completely confused and unsure of what to do next? I sure have many times. But the great news is that no matter how we feel, we never truly have to be stuck. We can look at the many different examples in God's Word. We can reflect on and reference the many different pictures of how Jesus handled a multitude of situations, and then respond the same way.

Trusting in Jesus' track record means adopting a willingness to also act it out in our own lives. It's easy to think about Jesus' words and actions. It's entirely different to abide in them and to live them out. Yet that's exactly what Jesus called each of us to do (John 8:31).

When we do this, it may initially feel unnatural for us. Others may disagree or even scoff at your decisions, your motives and your actions. You may encounter a multitude of additional challenges. You might even experience a wide range of negative and challenging emotions such as frustration, anger and doubt. I get it. I speak from experience. But know that all of this is okay. In a broken world, the truth will never feel comfortable. We can take comfort in knowing this from the get-go.

Trusting in God's track record means focusing even more intently on the bigger picture and the real goal behind it all. When we focus more intently on the final destination, it can help push everything we're currently struggling with to the sideline. It may not take it all away, but it can blur our focus on it, thus decreasing the intensity of its impact on us.

Purpose to keep the proper focus—on God, His ways and His track record and not on the persistent, nagging urge to control what was never ours to handle in the first place.

Embrace the role of manager, not master.

Look carefully then how you walk,
not as unwise but as wise,
making the best use of the time...
Ephesians 5:15-16a (ESV)

Talk is cheap. This also rings true in our walk with God. We can't just acknowledge God's role as Master in our lives and expect to see and to feel any real change. Our actions and our choices must also demonstrate it.

Please don't think I'm wagging my finger here. I'm not. I've struggled with this myself. I *still* do. As a recovering "Type A" personality, I couldn't wrap my head around the difference between wisely managing what God had put in my care and letting go of what was God's. To me, it was either being responsible or irresponsible, productive or lazy. I'd heard and even memorized the Serenity prayer: "...accept the things we cannot change, the courage to change the things we can, and the wisdom to know the difference." It's that last little part that always tripped me up in practice.

The day I got handed the massive list of over 370 different autosomal recessive genetic orders that Mark has markers for, is also the day I (honestly) wanted to crumple on the floor. It was undeniable evidence that no matter how much I tried, no matter how much medical advice I sought, no matter how much I tried to affect change, I simply couldn't fix Mark. And that was a tough and painful pill to swallow.

It's taken a bit of time to get to the point where I am now. Medically and cognitively speaking, Mark's grown much worse than the day we received the genetic news. He is now in constant joint pain, struggles with debilitating headaches and stomach pain and often struggles to string even two or three words together in any meaningful way.

But in another way—in a much more practical way—things are better. I've had to be very intentional about giving up the role of master that I so desperately wanted. I wanted to control and ultimately fix what wasn't mine to affect in the first place. But I had to completely let go of all of this in order to better focus on what I *could* do: manage the situation.

I could construct positive and fun distractions when the pain grew to be too much to bear. I could find and highlight joy when depression and defeat started to loom. I could be a steady support, funny sidekick and comforting companion to Mark. But I could only do all of this if I first gave up what was a losing battle to begin with. It's true. We need to pick our battles. Focus on knowing which ones are worth your time and effort.

I learned the hard (and exhausting) way that it's all about management versus mastery. It's that all-important wisdom which helps us to discern the difference accurately. We can—and should—manage ourselves, our actions, our reactions and our thoughts. We can even manage our choices, taking care to ensure they're in line with God's Word. But we can't control the outcome. Only the Master can do that (Proverbs 16:9, 20:24).

When we choose to trust in and wait on God, there's still plenty for us to do. Handing Him the wheel doesn't mean we sit idle. It means we change our focus from what's going on around us to what we can do within. By actively letting go of the control that was never truly ours in the first place, we free ourselves up to work on what we should—ourselves. Instead of reaching for the wheel, it's time to grab a mirror.

Practical Action:

I've admittedly struggled (greatly) to accept God's nurture over my own nature. It's not that I just don't *want* to let things go. It's that I fear doing so. But right there, in that very statement, lies the problem: fear. I can't love God perfectly—and relinquish all control to Him—if there's still fear casting shadows in my heart and head. None of us can. But fortunately, there is one thing that's already built-in to us that we can use to our advantage to help with this little—sometimes big—fear problem.

If you've ever been in a high-stress, emergency situation, you'll likely understand what I mean. Often in these kinds of circumstances, you really don't have time to think. You simply jump into busying yourself with what comes next—what has to be done—without even giving it much thought. We can employ this same knee-jerk reaction to action when it comes to managing, not mastering, our lives.

Whenever we sense fear or the urge to manage everything creeping in, we can lean into what we already know our priorities should be: becoming more like Jesus. When we allow ourselves to truly reflect on our personal and spiritual growth— including how far we still have yet to grow, a sense of urgency *should* come over us. And we can put this urgency to use for us. It can help us to focus on all of the important tasks that we should be busying ourselves with—making the best choices we can, working on our own spiritual growth and strengthening our relationship with God. Our plates should be so abundantly full with focusing on these that, frankly, we shouldn't have time to worry about much else. And this leads directly into the next point...

♡ Know there's never *not* stuff to do. Work on YOU!

Make every effort to respond to God's promises.
Supplement your faith with a generous provision of
moral excellence, and moral excellence with
knowledge, and knowledge with self-control,
and self-control with patient endurance,
and patient endurance with godliness.
2 Peter 1:5-6 (NLT)

As Mark has grown, so have his abilities and attentions. He can become completely obsessed with what's right and just. But he can do this to a fault. He has an unfortunate inclination to want to manage everyone around him instead of focusing on himself. Sometimes I can't help but laugh. He can be scolding someone for doing the exact same naughty thing he's currently doing at the exact same time. Ah, that's my little Mark!

It wasn't too long ago that I would become filled with fury over this. After all, those in glass houses shouldn't throw stones, right? But just recently a very important fact dawned on me. Well-meaning, capable-of-knowing-better adults do the *exact* same thing all the time! Sigh. Just like Mark, perhaps fewer of us would look like fools and be far more productive, if we spent less time worried about the affairs and actions of others and started managing our own selves instead.

We'd surely all still have plenty to keep us busy and occupied.

We can work on our thoughts and reactions. We can work on our personal knowledge and understanding of Scripture. We can work on our relationship with God, learning more about Him and using our fear and frustration as fuel to cling even tighter to Him. These are where we should focus our efforts. Our energy is never exerted in vain when we do these things. Save your energy. Save your sanity. Simply save yourself by giving everything else up.

℘ Practical Action:

There's a major difference between being self-focused and focusing on ourselves. The first is sinful. The Bible warns against pride over and over again (such as Proverbs 16:5, 18:12 and 21:4 just to name a few). But the latter is very important. Jesus Himself said, *"Hypocrite! First get rid of the log in your own eye..."* (Matthew 7:5a NLT). Without focusing on ourselves, we can't identify or work on our many flaws.

Still not convinced? Then think of it another way: Go gardening! Things don't happen accidentally, and neither does growing good fruit. If we want to allow the Holy Spirit room to grow good fruit in our lives (Galatians 5:22-23), then we need to be purposeful about not getting in the way. And this requires a certain amount of self-awareness and—yep, you guessed it—self-focus.

Be intentional about personal change and don't be scared to start small either. Jesus told us we shouldn't be. He told His disciples that faith so small—even as small as a tiny mustard seed—could do massive things (Luke 17:6). We can also apply this same truth to our own spiritual gardening.

Begin by identifying a specific behavior, feeling or reaction you'd like to change. Then, dissect it. *What exactly is it? What does it look like? What does it feel like?* Next, visualize the change you'd like to see. Don't skimp on the details. The more specific you are, the better able you will be to identify success when it comes. Finally, build a plan on how to get there and commit to making it happen. It's important to remind ourselves that having a map and *using* a map are two entirely different things. Our level of commitment to making change is what will actually get us there, not how sincere or heartfelt our intentions were at the beginning of the process.

Whatever you do, don't stop. Keep going! Promise yourself—and God—that you'll start over and over and over again as many times as it takes. Yes, it's important to own up to our failures. But growth never happens when we stay focused on them. We need to ask forgiveness from God and others when we screw up, and then fully accept the gift of that forgiveness. That means allowing ourselves to move on—without the weight of guilt holding us back—and committing to try harder as we move forward once again.

♡ Keep the urge to control in check.

There is a path before each person that seems right,
but it ends in death.
Commit everything you do to the LORD.
Trust him, and he will help you.
Proverbs 14:12, Psalm 37:5 (NLT)

"I eat this, Momma?"

"Yep!"

"You *sure?!*"

This is an all-too common conversation that I have with Mark. And I get it. He's worried and rightfully so. If he eats too much protein, he'll first suffer a horrible stomach ache. Next, will come the massive headache. Finally, he'll be struggling with crippling joint pain for the next few days. The kid's not stupid.

He's smart to be abundantly cautious.

But time and time again, I reassure Mark that I worry so that he doesn't have to. His low IQ keeps him from being able to count and keep track of the total grams of protein in each item. His short and long term memory loss hinder him from keeping a running total of his daily protein consumption. But he doesn't need to worry. He doesn't have to try and control everything he eats because I do it for him.

"Everything I give you and everything I put on your plate you can eat," I reassure him with a smile. "You can trust me." And with that, relief washes across his face and food gets shoved into his mouth.

Trusting God with every aspect of our lives isn't a one-time event. It's an ongoing choice, just like Mark has to choose to trust me at each and every meal. It won't feel natural at first. That's because giving up control can leave us feeling helpless. It reminds us of how very little control we really do have. And that can be scary, *very* scary. Yikes.

Parenting a child with a mountain of ever-changing medical, developmental and physical special needs can admittedly sometimes leave me feeling like I simply can't catch my breath. The weight of my worry can quite literally knock the wind right out of me. Other times, I feel like I'm drowning in a sea of unknowns, running away with worry about what the future may—and in a lot of ways, may not—hold for Mark and our family. But that's when I check myself and stop focusing on the tumultuous waters all around me.

God has promised that we are never alone (Psalm 23:4, 139:7-10). He promises to direct our paths (Proverbs 3:6) and to help and strengthen us (Psalm 28:7). God even promises perfect peace if only we'll trust in Him (Isaiah 26:3). But none of this just magically happens. Our relationship with God can forever keep us in the peaceful, safe, silent eye of the storm. But this doesn't just happen. We have to purpose to stay there in order to make it so.

The next time you find yourself grasping for control or feeling a bit like you're gasping for air under the weight of your burdens, take a tip from Peter. Keep your focus on Jesus. Don't let the storm distract your focus, no matter how it may whip and whirl around. In fact, I'll bet Noah would echo that same sentiment. When the storm hits, it's not time to jump ship. It's time to cling even tighter to it. So let the wind blow. Cling to the Anchor you already know is there.

Practical Action:

Imagine how Noah must have felt on that ark. Bobbing around on the water in a boat with no mode of navigation. He couldn't steer the thing even if he wanted to. And just imagine all the noise that must have surrounded him. The sounds of so many animals—large and small—all around him and the sound of beating rain as it pelted against the large wooden structure. I imagine Noah must've stuck his head out the window more than a time or two to look up at the sky, wondering when the rain would stop. Perhaps he reminded himself, too, that God still had His protective eye on him.

We can also keep our own urge to control in check by giving ourselves a little "know like Noah" moment from time to time. We can look at all the confusing, crazy stuff going on around us and take pause in the middle of it to remember who was, is and will continue to be in control of it all (Isaiah 45:7). And if things feel completely out of our control, that's probably because they are. Remember Noah on the ark—the massive boat *without* navigation. Let the chaos and crazy be while you ride it out. Know your role. Noah it just like Noah did.

⌘ Manage your emotions.

A man without self-control
is like a city broken into and left without walls.
Proverbs 25:28 (ESV)

My little guy can be a complete emotional mess. It's amazing. His mood can turn on a dime. One minute he can be smiling and laughing and the next he can be a sad, slobbery mess incapable of speaking at all.

Mark was like this from the very beginning, including before he had any words in his vocabulary. It was very evident to me that Mark could comprehend far more than he could express. It soon became clear that he could also feel much more than he could explain, even to himself.

But I had to do something. I knew there was probably no way to take away these powerful emotions. I'd been smart enough to figure out that many of them stemmed from hurts he'd experienced in the past, which I didn't know about. I also figured that much of his anger was actually just extreme frustration.

He would repeatedly become angry with himself. He couldn't always remember things when he wanted to. He was terribly slow when he wanted to do things quickly. Even when he was able to say a word correctly, as soon as it left his lips he often realized it wasn't the right word at all. This would add up to a tremendous amount of frustration—and even anger—for anyone. Yet here it was. It was all trapped inside of a little boy who could barely talk. I couldn't take all the challenges of his special needs away. But there had to be *some* way to help him better navigate and cope.

Practice doesn't make perfect, but it does make progress. And that's what Mark and I made together. We spent many, *many* hours on his bed in the privacy of his room exploring his feelings—and his reactions—together. I talked calmly and quietly regardless of how much he screamed, sweat and spit. I used words to describe his actions and purposefully attached them to the feelings he was experiencing inside. I intentionally tried to give labels to the emotions he was struggling with, even when he couldn't. All of this validated what he was going through. Often it was enough to just be heard even when he didn't know how or what he wanted to say. And all of this helped.

Self-control isn't about not feeling or experiencing emotions. It's about how we respond to them and how we manage them. The Apostle Paul said, *"Be angry and do not sin"* (Ephesians 4:26 ESV). He didn't admonish the emotion. Instead, he gave clear instructions on how to respond to it.

Even Jesus felt the wealth of emotions we all struggle with (Hebrews 4:15). We can know this because He was fully human (Galatians 4:4-5). The Gospel writers did a wonderful job sharing even the emotional details of Jesus' life. And we can take a lot of comfort from this.

Jesus felt anger (Mark 3:5). He felt indignation (Mark 10:14). He even felt troubled (John 13:21). Knowing this should help us feel less surprised about our own wide range of sometimes perplexing and often powerful emotions.

We can also learn from Christ's example on how to respond appropriately. We can follow His lead and know that it's okay to allow ourselves to feel. Jesus didn't avoid, deny or stuff His emotions down. (Want proof? Just look up one of the shortest verses of the Bible: John 11:35.)

So strive not to be a stuffer. Instead, take time to pull even the most confounding and most shameful emotion into the spotlight. By not allowing it to bubble below the surface or flirt around the fringes of your daily interactions (even with yourself), you can strip the emotion of its power. Like fear, the control that emotions have over us is limited. It's limited to the amount of control that we allow them to have. It's not about not feeling. It's not about not experiencing emotions. It's about managing them so they don't manage us.

🐾 Practical Action:

Einstein once said, "Any fool can know. The point is to understand." We can know a lot of things. We can know right from wrong. We can know why we made particular choices. We can even know how we feel. But the latter really doesn't really matter unless we understand *why* we feel the way that we do. If we can get to the why, then we have a much better chance of figuring out exactly how to manage it. In short, we can respond rather than react.

A reaction is knee-jerk, a reflex and a nearly instantaneous effect of some cause. A response, on the other hand, is much more involved. It requires thought, critical thinking and understanding. I'm purposeful in giving Mark the time, privacy and space he needs in order to work through his feelings and come to an appropriate and positive response. We can and should do this for ourselves too. Breathing room is important, but so is *feeling* room—intentional space in between an event and our response.

We live in a world where speed is prized, including

making decisions and doling out reactions. But how much better off— and more authentic and honest—could we all be if we only reserved our right to a delayed response. It's *okay* to take a minute (or two or twenty!) to sort out how you truly feel and why. This step is not only okay, it's absolutely essential for effective emotional management.

Don't believe me? Take your cue from Christ instead. The scribes and Pharisees once brought a woman caught committing adultery to Jesus in the hopes of trying to test him. They were purposefully trying to trap him into a particular reaction so they could condemn him (John 8:1-6a). But Jesus didn't fall for it. Despite the small crowd of all those gathered—undoubtedly waiting with baited breath for His response—Jesus didn't succumb to the pressure. He didn't speak. He didn't utter a single sound. Instead, Jesus bent down and wrote with his finger on the ground (John 8:6b ESV).

It is understandable that considerable curiosity swirls around what Jesus might have actually written in the sand that day. But Scripture doesn't tell us, so perhaps what He wrote isn't what's important at all. Instead, maybe the lesson lies in *how* Jesus responded: calmly and in His timing.

When we reflect on this and apply it to our own day-to-day lives, we better appreciate that it's okay to take the time we need in order to better respond in a way that's thought out and intentional. We can also know that we're in the absolute best company when we do so: Jesus.

Jesus took the space He wanted by bending. He literally distanced Himself from all the others standing around staring at Him. He also occupied Himself with an activity of His choosing—writing. We can follow this same two-step example. We can purpose to give ourselves the space to sort out, reflect on and ultimately manage our emotions.

Finally, we can find concrete ways to do all of these things. For some, it may mean turning to a trusted friend to talk. For others, it might mean finding quiet time alone. For still others, it might mean writing just like Jesus did, maybe in a journal or even just in list form. The way we do it isn't important. Following His perfect example is.

ABOUT SHANNON

Shannon Medisky is a leading expert in struggling with stress, screwing up and seeking God in the midst of it all.

Sometimes funny but always real, Shannon's writing is infused with practical ideas grounded in God's Word to help others create positive, real change in their daily lives.

Follow Shannon's blog, discover new resources and join in the conversation at ShannonMedisky.com.

Looking for more books and resources like this one that share practical, concrete ways to apply God's Word to your life today?

Then visit ShannonMedisky.com where you'll discover new ways to *grow* on, not just go on.

Dear Reader,
I'm different from a lot of writers because I don't write about what I know. Instead, I write about what I desperately need to learn. And I'm honored that you've joined me on this journey by reading this book.

Do you have questions, comments or suggestions? Or just want to say, "Hi?" I'd love to hear from you! You can connect with me through email or via social media at ShannonMedisky.com.

Yours because we're His,

Shannon